The Byzantine Empire

The Middle Ages Ancient History of Europe

Children's Ancient History

The Byzantine Empire, centered on the city in Turkey that was called Constantinople and is now called Istanbul, was one of the longest-lived empires in history.

It started as part of the Roman Empire, became the "new Rome", and survived long after its parent empire had fallen apart. Read on and learn the story of the Byzantine Empire, or Byzantium.

BYZANTINE ARCHITECTURE

From Colony to Part of an Empire

The Roman world expanded from a small settlement in Italy to a republic that controlled much of what is now Italy and western Europe. As it continued to expand, it became an Empire and eventually controlled the lands all around the Mediterranean Sea, as far north as Scotland and as far east as Iran.

This expansion was not into empty lands. Rome conquered and absorbed ancient and complex civilizations, including Egypt, Gaul, and the Greek city-states.

ROMAN FORUM

Among the many cities added to the Roman Empire was Byzantium, a Greek colony on the shore of the Bosphorus channel that connects the Mediterranean with the Black Sea. Byzantium was small, but it had a great location both for trade and for defence in time of war. It had been on the border of the Greek and Persian worlds, although both sides of the Bosphorus were now rich parts of the Roman Empire.

TWO ROMAN EMPIRES

In time, the Roman Empire grew too big, and faced challenges from too many directions, for all the decisions to be made in Rome. In 330 C.E. the Emperor Constantine established Byzantium, which he renamed Constantinople after himself, as the eastern capital of the Empire.

SIEGE OF CONSTANTINOPLE

In 364 Emperor Valentian I formally divided the Empire into eastern and western sections, with his brother Valens as Emperor of the East in Constantinople. The two sections were one when facing external enemies, but began to grow apart as their interests, challenges, and opportunities differed. The western Empire was now mainly on the defensive against waves of attacks by migrating peoples from northern and eastern Europe, while the eastern Empire was becoming the most powerful force in its part of the world.

In 476, Odoacer overthrew the last Roman Emperor and proclaimed himself King of Italy. This was the end of the Roman Empire in the west.

Learn more about the western empire in the Baby Professor book Everything You Need to Know about the Rise and Fall of the Roman Empire.

POWERFUL BYZANTIUM

Byzantium continued and even grew stronger. It had shorter supply lines to its frontiers, a shorter border to defend against the European migrations, and great resources from the riches of western Asia and the Middle East that it organized and deployed well.

ALEXANDER THE GREAT

Although the Eastern Empire inherited Roman law and political structures, and Latin was its official language in its first centuries, it became more and more a culture of Greek traditions and language. Many of Byzantium's strongest emperors and military leaders came from Macedonia in Greece, and you could say they continued the traditions and success of the Macedonian Alexander the Great.

Justinian I became emperor in 527 and ruled until 565. His armies conquered much of North Africa and other parts of the former western empire. Justinian's court revised Roman law into the Byzantine legal and government system that would last for almost a thousand years and establish the basis of modern government.

JUSTINIAN 1

The Byzantine Empire was at the height of its power. However, it had built up huge debts to pay for its armies and other developments, and taxes rose sharply throughout the Empire. This slowed down the development of business in various regions, and even caused local revolts that the central government had to put down.

Byzantium tried to hold on to more territory than its armies could control and defend—the same problem the Roman Empire had faced. Attacks by Persians in the east and Slavs in the west combined with internal rebellions to strain and shrink the empire.

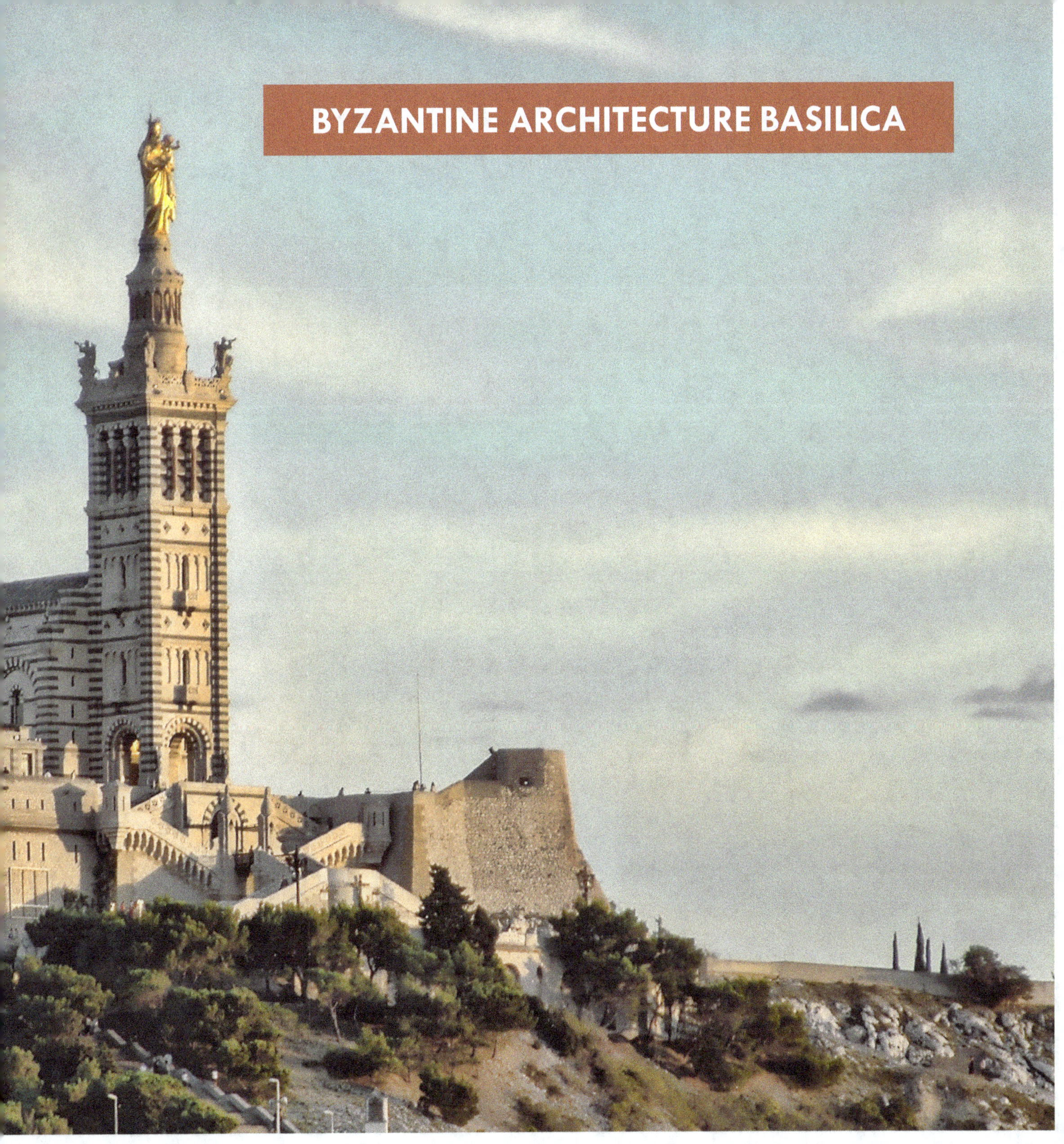
BYZANTINE ARCHITECTURE BASILICA

However, the biggest challenge turned out to be the rise of Islam in Arabia. The armies of Islam grappled with the armies of Byzantium across a wide front, gradually winning away from the Empire all of North Africa and much of the Middle East.

CRISIS OF POWER

In the 11th century Byzantium was under attack from both the Muslim armies and forces from the East. The Empire appealed to the western kingdoms for help, and under the Pope the West launched a series of Crusades that, over the next 200 years, tried to take back the "Holy Land" (where Israel, Lebanon, and Jordan now are) from the Muslims.

Some of these efforts succeeded for a while. But far too soon the leaders from the West started quarrelling with Byzantium over who should benefit from territory gained and victories won. In 1204 the Fourth Crusade turned from its plans to fight to gain the Holy Land, and attacked and captured Constantinople. Byzantium eventually recaptured the city, but it was much weakened by fighting with its allies at the same time as continuing to fight the Muslim forces and the Seljuk Turks pushing in from the east.

THE LONG FALL

From the middle of the 13th century, the effect of so many wars, against so many enemies, was cripplng the Byzantine Empire. It basically had no money to continue the services its people needed and also pay for its many armies.

After a long struggle, Byzantium became a client kingdom, paying tribute to the Turkish Ottoman Empire. Periodially in the 14th century the situation got better, but the general trend was downward. Byzantium continued to lose territories and power, and to spend resources it could not afford on battles it could not win. Toward the end, the Byzantine Empire controlled very little territory outside of the city of Constantinople itself.

Finally, in the 1420s, the Ottoman Turks revoked all treaties with Byzantium and set out to destroy the Empire. And even then, it took 40 years before Constantinople finally fell!

LIFE IN BYZANTIUM

People in the west used to have a negative image of the Byzantine Empire. They saw it as corrupt and pleasure-seeking, with its rulers more interested in luxury than in ruling. This is very far from the truth.

For most of its thousand-year life, the Byzantine Empire had political and military leaders who were generally competent and energetic. If they had not been good at their jobs, the Empire would not have lasted a year, much less a thousand!

6034 Z - CONSTANTINOPLE LA PLACE EMIN-ONOU ET YENI DJAMI

The central government was a strong patron of the arts, from painting and poetry to magnificant churches, towers, and other structures. Although taxes were high to pay for the constant wars, the government made sure business could function and goods could get from city to city. People in cities had access to education and many career opportunities, and there were many hospitals and doctors. Scholars studied and preserved the wisdom of Greek philosophers and scientists.

Things were tougher in rural areas, of course, and in areas near where armies were fighting. The goal for many was to get to a city for greater options, even if it meant joining the army and spending a career as a soldier.

ORTHODOX CHURCH

RELIGOUS IMPACT

The Byzantine Empire was strongly Christian, but its understanding of God and how Christians should live developed in a slightly different way from in the Western Empire. Crises developed over whether it was right to display and pray to images of God and the saints, and over details as small as a single word in the Creed, the statement of what Christians believe. Eventually Christianity developed two major sections: in the West, Christians were part of the Holy Catholic Church under the Pope, the bishop of Rome. In the East, a series of patriarchs guided what became known as the Orthodox Church.

Over the centuries, people have fought and killed each other over this separation, from the Crusaders onward. Now the major parts of Christianity work in better cooperation and more in the spirit of the teachings of Christ.

ΑΙΝΩΝΕΝΘΑ
ΝΥΝΟCΑΠΠCΑ
ΦΑC
ΒΕΘΑΒΑΡΑ
ΤΟΤΥΑΓΙΩΙΩΑΝΝΟΥ
ΤΥΒΑ ΠΤΙCΜΑ
ΤΟC
ΑΚΩΝΑΘΑΝΑΓΜ
ΒΗΘΑΓΛΑ
ΓΑΛΓΑΛΑΤΟΚΑΙΓ
ΔΩΔΕΚΑΛΙΘΟΝ
ΙΕΡΙΧΩ
ΑΡΧΕΛΑΙC ΤΟΤΥΑΓΙΩ
ΛΕΥΙΑ ΕΛΙCΑΙΟΥ

THE LEGACY OF THE EMPIRE

Even as the Byzantine Empire declined politically and as a miliary force, its cultural influence grew and spread. Byzantine scentists and artists influenced work and research both in Europe and in the Middle East. When Constantinople finally fell, many scholars and artists moved to western capitals and worked in European countries. They brought with them manuscripts from classical Greek times, and many writings from the early Christian era, that helped strengthen and speed up Europe's move out of the "dark ages".

The religious influence of the Eastern Orthodox Church continues among Christians in many countries, including Greece, Russia, Romania, Bulgaria, and Serbia.

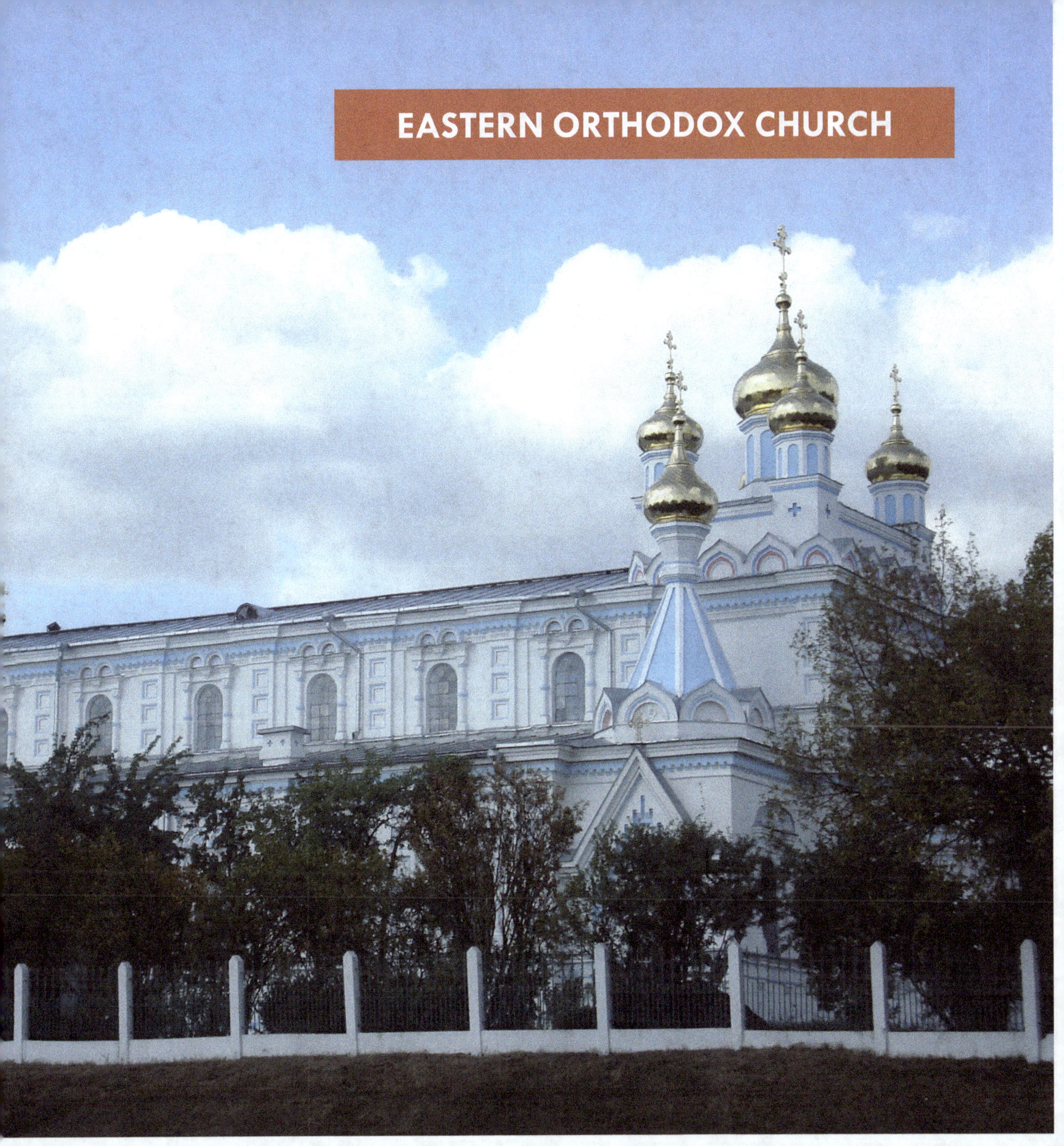

EASTERN ORTHODOX CHURCH

THE PAST SUPPORTS OUR PRESENT

The Byzantine Empire began about 1500 years ago and lasted for a thousand years. Only the Chinese empire had a longer continuous reign. The Byzantine Empire helped to form the world we live in now, both political structures and a sense of what makes effective government.

What other empires and kingdoms influenced how we live today?

Read further in Baby Professor books like Who Were the Barbarians? for some surprising answers.

MACEDONIAN ART (BYZANTINE)

Visit
BABY PROFESSOR
EDUCATION KIDS
www.BabyProfessorBooks.com
to download Free Baby Professor eBooks
and view our catalog of new and exciting
Children's Books